Re-Creations
Visualizing O

D0537445

Mark Redknap

Contents

Introduction

The archaeologist and historian are both scientists and artists. Their first aim is to seek objective truth and to debunk anything false, but they seek, as does the artist, to illumine the truth with imagination.

Rt Hon. Lord Harlech, 1949 (President of the National Museum of Wales 1937–42)

Have you ever imagined what a long-abandoned settlement and its inhabitants once looked like? The further we go back in time, the more we have to visualize the past through re-creations. This is usually the last stage of a puzzle-solving process which resembles detective work: finding clues and piecing together evidence to reconstruct what happened in the past. This analogy between criminal detection and archaeology has long been recognized by many writers, including Wilkie Collins, Sir Arthur Conan Doyle and Agatha Christie, who wrote: 'You would have made a good archaeologist, M. Poirot. You have the gift of re-creating the past' (*Murder in Mesopotamia* 1936 (1979), 188). Archaeology is constantly causing us to reassess our view of the past, either through new discoveries or the application of new techniques. It produces evidence of people's lives through the ages and draws on our imagination to bridge the centuries.

Archaeological reconstruction can involve many different techniques – paintings, illustrations, models, replicas, restorations, re-enactments, facial reconstructions and 'virtual reality' computer visualization. All of these methods can help place the complex mass of archaeological evidence into a physical and social context which can be easily understood by the non-specialist. This book outlines some of these methods and shows how our ideas of the past are under constant revision.

The examples of reconstructed scenes shown here range in date from early prehistory to the early seventeenth century. Many have been commissioned by organizations which play a key role in the interpretation of the archaeology and historic sites of Wales. Some have been created for the National Museums & Galleries of Wales from the 1930s onwards to inform visitors about archaeological sites in Wales. Others are a selection of those researched and commissioned by Cadw: Welsh Historic Monuments from the mid-1980s to illustrate their site guidebooks and on-site interpretation displays. Other bodies, such as the Royal Commission on the Ancient and Historical Monuments of Wales and the four Welsh Archaeological Trusts, also make extensive use of archaeological reconstruction to help bring the past to life.

Working sketch by Tony Daly (pencil and ink, 1995) with annotations for an imaginative view of a burial dating from some 4,000 years ago. During the Early Bronze Age, the deceased was placed in a crouched position in a slab-lined grave. In the grave of an important man were placed those items required in the next world. Such illustrations can give the bare archaeological evidence a more explicit human context.

Dolwyddelan Castle, Conwy, as it might have appeared in the later thirteenth century, by Chris Jones-Jenkins (watercolour and ink, 1994). The castle was built by Llywelyn ab Iorwerth about 1210–40. The drawing was first prepared in ink on tracing film, then copied onto watercolour paper prior to colouring. (Cadw)

Reconstruction of the main entrance to the Iron Age hillfort at Llanmelin, Monmouthshire, by Alan Sorrell (1940). Art in the service of archaeology need not lack intensity of visual expression and vitality, and this scene at the entrance to the hillfort uses animated groups of figures to create imaginary incidents.
(National Museum of Wales)

A Developing Medium

This French manuscript illustration of the construction of the Tower of Babel, from the early fifteenth-century La Bible Hystoriaulx, *demonstrates how the past was imagined by the medieval mind in terms of the 'present': contemporary medieval dress, building styles and methods of construction. (British Library Royal 15 DIII fol. 15v)*

Without drawing or designing the Study of Antiquitys or any other Science is lame and imperfect.

Reverend William Stukeley (1687–1765), Minute-Book of the Society of Antiquaries of London, after 1725 (Society of Antiquaries MS 268, fol. 2r)

Historical reconstruction has a very long pedigree; it is rooted in the visual art of medieval Europe, and the mythological, religious and historical imagery of this period. Illustrators then, as now, were influenced by the sway of artistic conventions and the degree of understanding of the subject. During the Middle Ages, the past was seen in terms of the present, through the Bible, chronicles and narratives. Illustrations of the legendary King Arthur from a twelfth-century copy of Geoffrey of Monmouth's *History of the Kings of Britain* and later medieval miniatures featuring episodes from the Arthurian romances show contemporary rather than historic detail. It was only in the fifteenth century that differences between periods began to be recognized. The tradition of applying higher standards of accuracy in painting classical subjects through the study of antiquities was established during the Renaissance. Discoveries during the eighteenth century, such as those at Herculaneum (from 1711) and Pompeii (from 1748), promoted even greater precision. The legacy of earlier representations and conventions, and the conditioning of the imagination can be charted through different versions of the same scene.

Many early images were often better reflections of the society in which they were produced than of the past they represented, as can be seen in early depictions of 'prehistoric' life. Until the development of a greater understanding of prehistory, artists relied largely on classical sources. Biblical iconography, such as the medieval versions of our creation ancestry, was highly influential and provided a model for the appearance of prehistoric man. Renaissance artists contributed to an iconography of early origins with powerful, made-up portrayals of classical Greek and Roman myths of our development. Many nineteenth-century illustrators were influenced by a desire to chart the progress of western civilization from rough, crude, barbaric savages – characterized by traditional artistic conventions such as animal skin garments, semi-nakedness, clubs, hunched postures and cave dwellings – through to their own times. The image of the barbarian warrior as 'noble savage' was influential, and the rise of Darwin's evolutionary theory during the nineteenth century was initially accompanied by the adoption of ape-like images for early humans. By the end of the century, historical awareness had increased and new information from archaeologists, ethnographers and antiquaries began to make an increasing contribution, though interpretations based on the same data could still widely differ.

Adam and Eve, from the Nuremberg Chronicle *(woodcut, 1483). According to the Bible, God created both as fully formed human beings. Medieval images of them after their expulsion from the Garden of Eden often show Adam working the land, and a clothed Eve, resembling the Virgin Mary, nurturing infants. (British Library I.C. 7452)*

Woodcut of the Welsh prince Llywelyn ap Gruffudd (about 1225–82), dressed in Roman armour. In the absence of portraits, many artists drew on the same stock of warrior images, often with anachronistic details of weapons and clothing. This example appears to be based on the wood engraving of Llywelyn in David Powel's The Historie of Cambria (1584). (National Museum of Wales)

'Ancient Britons', by Lucas de Heere (watercolour, about 1575), shows the use of body paint, long shields, a spear taken from classical sources and an anachronistic sword. From his Corte Beschryvinghe van England, Scotlande, ende Irland (1660). (British Library, Add. MS 28330)

Aquatint by Robert Havell of 'A Briton of the Interior' from Samuel Rush Meyrick and Charles Hamilton Smith, The Costume of the Original Inhabitants of the British Islands, from the earliest periods to the sixth century *(London, 1815). This is an early example of incorporating archaeological detail: the 'noble barbarian savage' is equipped with a Bronze Age shield, socketed axe and rapier mounted as a spear. (National Museum of Wales)*

'Archer and Crossbowman AD 1250', from the publication by Sir Samuel Rush Meyrick (1783–1848) entitled A Critical Inquiry into Antient Armour as it Existed in Europe, but particularly in England from the Norman Conquest to the Reign of King Charles II *(London, 1824). Meyrick's main aim was to establish a chronology for armour, and to introduce 'into paintings and scenic representations of all kinds an historical correctness with which our ancestors were acquainted'. (National Museum of Wales)*

HISTORY PAINTING

Like the historian, the history painter must narrate general truths, by vivid representation of particular facts … he must place our ancestors before us in all the peculiarities of their dress and time until they seem … beings of flesh and blood.

Art Union, 1843

From the mid-eighteenth century, British artists were being influenced by literature and the antiquarian study of artefacts, dress, portraiture, sculpture, architecture and furniture. Painters began to place medieval characters within their correct historic environments, and publications such as the engravings in Joseph Strutt's *Complete View of the Dress and Habits of the People of England* (1796–99) provided valuable source material. The Society of Antiquaries encouraged the examination of the 'Relickes of former Ages', and during the eighteenth and early nineteenth centuries included many influential artists, architects and sculptors among its Fellows. The portraits by engravers such as George Vertue (1684–1756) and Welshman, Robert Vaughan (worked about 1622–66), provided historical painters with sources for more accurate likenesses. Artists now realized that they could enable the public to 'witness' famous historic events.

Eighteenth-century cultural theory held that 'history' painting was the highest form of art in which artists could be involved, as reflected in the prizes offered for historical subjects by the Royal Academy (founded 1768). The content of such images was very different from today, for until about 1820 architecture and natural beauty, antiquities and the picturesque were all considered to be one in the minds of many. Artists such as Benjamin West (1728–1820), Richard Wilson (1713–82) and his pupil, Thomas Jones (1742–1803), visualized scenes from literature and poetry set in the past. Benjamin West, principal history painter to George III (1760–1820), engendered a shift on convention within history painting. Instead of figures dressed in classical robes placed before idealized scenery, West depicted incidents set against recognizable locations with figures in contemporary dress. Defending his idea of conveying history plainly, rather than allegorically, he stated: 'The same truth that guides the pen of the historian should govern the pencil of the artist'. As artists extended the scope of their subject matter, they became more concerned with accuracy in depicting dress.

The publication in 1814 of *Waverley* by Sir Walter Scott (1771–1832) heralded another genre, the 'Intimate Romantic' paintings, which provided glimpses of domestic scenes from earlier ages. The various illustrated editions of Scott's historical novels had great impact on historical painting, and included work by Robin Scott Lauder (1803–69) and the 'Scottish' school of historical painters. Walter Scott extended the subject range of the history painters by using everyday people and events: 'the bygone ages of the world were actually filled with living men, not by protocols, state papers, controversies and abstractions'. Scott's historical writings produced a wealth of related paintings, prints, illustrated books and costume design.

Following the popular unrest of the early nineteenth century in the wake of the French Revolution, national history and ancestry became important issues in Britain. From the 1830s onwards, the public required art to make the past live again in the present. Society was trying to make sense of the rapid economic and social changes brought about by the Agricultural and Industrial Revolutions, and history painting provided a mirror in which contemporary life could be studied and explained. The paintings depicted a relevant and useful past: usually great events from literature, history or the Bible, in imaginary settings. The Victorian view of the past evoked visions of heroes and heroines, of stories and legends. Some artists, such as Ford Madox Brown (1821–93), used medieval dress to bring the past alive; other painters were more concerned with creating Romantic settings. Historical scenes had the power to grip the imagination, blending history, romance and patriotism, so that by the 1850s, the heroes and heroines of British history were well known to most and their lessons supported imperial aspirations of the time.

King René's honeymoon, by Ford Madox Brown (1864; oil, NMW A171). Designed as an ornamental panel for a drawing desk, it depicts a scene from the imagined honeymoon of King René of Anjou (1408–1480), the famous fifteenth-century patron of the arts and father of Margaret, queen to King Henry VI (1422–61). The panel illustrates 'Architecture', and the king is shown pointing to details on a plan of the palace he is building. From a nineteenth-century perspective, the Middle Ages were seen as an idyllic period of security and order. In the interests of accuracy, Ford Madox Brown not only studied historical dress, using sources such as Henry Shaw's Dress and Decoration of the Middle Ages *(written in the 1840s), but also made his own replica costumes. (National Museum of Wales)*

Detail from The Bard *by Thomas Jones (1774). One of his most successful early works, he was, like other artists, inspired by Thomas Gray's 'Pindaric Ode',* The Bard *(1757). Jones has visualized its subject, the legendary massacre of Welsh bards by King Edward I (1272–1307) after his conquest of Wales in 1282 - 83. The bearded bard is set in a mountain landscape surrounded by the remains of an earlier 'Celtic' past. He represents native stock, and the Welsh as upholders of ancient 'British' stock. For similar reasons, the English heroine Boudicca, first-century queen of the Iceni, had a particular resonance in Wales, 'home of the language in which she thought and spoke'. (National Museum of Wales)*

The Death of Tewdrig, *by John Evan and William Meredyth Thomas (bronze, 1848), an early example of historical sculpture. Tewdrig was a fifth- or sixth-century king of Gwent, who is thought to have been killed fighting the pagan English. The costume of the king and his daughter, Merchell, is eleventh- to thirteenth-century in style. (National Museum of Wales)*

*Illustration by James Finnemore from a
version of the Icelandic saga* Kormak the Viking
*(J. F. Hodgetts, 1902). The icon of the winged
or horned Viking helmet, for which there
is no archaeological evidence, has a long and
persistent history. (National Museum of Wales)*

ILLUSTRATION AND FILM

By 1865, many artists had begun to find antiquarian authenticity suffocating. During the late nineteenth century some of them returned to purely pictorial values in painting, and moved away from historical illustration. By the end of the century, re-creating the past had become largely the field of the illustrator, theatre designer and eventually the film director. From the late nineteenth century, specialist artists were employed by publishers to produce graphic reconstructions, with an emphasis on accuracy.

The invention of lithography (a process of printing from stone) led to the mass-production of cheap illustrations. The *Illustrated London News* published high-quality paintings and engravings, and established a reputation for reporting archaeological discoveries with images of objects and excavations in progress, as well as dramatic reconstructions. The figure and landscape painter and illustrator, Amedée Forestier (1854–1930), worked for the *Illustrated London News* from 1882, and from 1900 devoted himself to archaeological illustration and presenting new discoveries to a wide readership. Some of his later work was aimed to provide students, writers and actors with 'documentary value' information on appearance. The dominance of the *Illustrated London News* was eventually challenged by the growth of photographic reproduction at the beginning of the twentieth century. By this time, far more people from a broader spectrum of society than ever before were interested in the past. This was reflected by the growth of the state provision for education, museums and art galleries.

Our perceptions about the past tend to be influenced from an early age by illustrations in books as well as by films, dramatic productions, creative literature and poetry. For over 400 years, Shakespeare's history plays have transported audiences back in time, and have been an introduction to a past with real people. This impact was extended to a wider audience through the publication of engravings of scenes from the plays, such as those engraved by J. Fettler, based on paintings by John Opie (1761–1807). Books for children, in particular, continue to benefit from a wealth of stock scenes, many of which are powerful and have become icons of the past. For example, some of Forestier's work was still being used to illustrate children's history books as late as 1970, as well as providing a basis for reconstructions in the 1980s. Such images and associated accounts, absorbed at an impressionable age, have had a lasting influence on our perception of the past.

Early twentieth-century films were seen as a progression from lithography and photography, and a move towards more realistic representations. They heralded the possibility of reconstructing the past with greater realism, and many recognized their potential to 'narrate' history. For their early promoters and for many audiences, historical films were 'true' histories. They were very popular, and often contained memorable scenes which appeared to epitomize a particular period or event. Many set in the classical world were influenced by artists and designers such as Jean-Léon Gérôme (1824–1904) and Sir Lawrence Alma-Tadema (1836–1912). Some early films used historic sites as sets: the silent version of Sir Walter Scott's *Ivanhoe* by the Imperial Film Company (1913) was shot on location at Chepstow Castle.

IDEAL SKETCH OF A SWISS LAKE-DWELLING.
"Restored" from the latest discoveries.

Frontispiece from Ferdinand Keller's The Lake Dwellings of Switzerland and Other Parts of Europe *(translated by John Edward Lee, 1866). The influence of such work extended beyond archaeology. This reconstruction may have inspired J. R. R. Tolkien's Lake Town, Esgaroth, in* The Hobbit *(1937). (National Museum of Wales)*

Glastonbury Iron Age Lake Village, Somerset, by Amedée Forestier (watercolour on paper, 1911). This reconstruction was based on the excavations by Arthur Bulleid and Harold St George Gray between 1892 and 1907. It was produced for an article by Arthur Bulleid entitled 'Not the Woad-daubed Savage of Old History Books: the Civilised Ancient Briton' in the Illustrated London News. *The figures are drawn from late nineteenth-century romantic representations of ancient Gaulish warriors. Much of the equipment is of an incorrect period, being of later Bronze Age date. The helmet worn by the chieftain resembles a north Italian (Villanovan) crested helmet and the sword copies 'Tarquinian' swords of the same date. The current view is that there would have been fewer roundhouses at any one time, and that the site was occupied about 200–50 BC. (Somerset County Council Museums Service)*

Illustration can also provide human context. This imaginary scene, by Victor Ambrus (b. 1935), is of an historic episode in the boyhood of William Marshal (c.1147–1219), who eventually became earl of Pembroke. King Stephen threatened to hang his youthful hostage in sight of his father, whose castle he was besieging. The picture was created by Victor Ambrus in 1989 for an interpretation panel at Chepstow Castle, Monmouthshire. He characterizes his work as realistic, decorative and strongly influenced by his training as an etcher. 'People are important to me – after all, there would be no buildings, artefacts, or settlements without them. I love drawing reconstructions of what people looked like, what they did, what they wore, how they behaved'. (Cadw)

The Fortress Baths at Caerleon. This early computer-generated image, created by the School of Engineering, University of Bath (1983), gives an impression of the bath building across the exercise yard (palaestra). (National Museum of Wales)

Whatever the care taken in set designs, costumes and props, the scripts were fiction and many often failed in their accurate portrayal of detail. In this sense, Cecil B. DeMille's *The Sign of the Cross* (1932) and *Cleopatra* (1934), Stanley Kubrick's *Spartacus* (1960) and Anthony Mann's *The Fall of the Roman Empire* (1964) remain products of their time.

As computer processing speed continues to increase and graphic quality steadily improves, so developments in computer visualization, from photo-realistic graphics through to multimedia and virtual reality, are now being used more readily to present reconstructions. These can range from predefined or interactive 'flythrough' paths through or around structures, to the placing of an individual within an artificial environment, where past worlds can be seen and 'heard', or the digital re-creation of sites and scenes on film, such as Rome and the Colosseum in the film *Gladiator* (2000). An early example created for on-site interpretation in the mid-1980s was a computer-generated model of the Fortress Baths at the Roman legionary fortress, Caerleon. For this, a three-dimensional geometric description was created, and then rendering methods were used to provide surface colours, textures and lighting. Improvements in both hardware and software now make much more sophisticated images possible. Digital measurements can be imported into a computer to create a 'wire frame', which then has successive layers of detail added to build up a realistic image. Unlike physical models, such computer-generated models are extremely flexible. They can have mobile viewpoints, be rotated, scaled up and down, and allow the viewer to travel around the scene.

REVIVALS

If things go on at this rate, not only our churches, but our studies and our drawing rooms will be older than they were five hundred years ago.

The Times, 2 June, 1862 (commenting on the Victorian Gothic of the International Exhibition)

Cardiff Castle in the fourteenth century, by John Ward (watercolour and ink on paper, about 1911). Ward, curator of the Cardiff Museum and Art Gallery and from 1912 first Keeper of Archaeology at the National Museum of Wales, completed the recording of archaeological discoveries made during the alterations taking place at the castle, following G. T. Clark's death in 1898. It shows features completed by the early fourteenth century under the de Clare earls (1217–1314). The Black Tower is thirteenth century, and the shell keep twelfth century. An unfinished drawing by Ward of the Norman castle has been found on the reverse. (National Museum of Wales)

It was not only in the two-dimensional field of pictorial illustration that developments were taking place. By the eighteenth century, antiquarianism was exerting a strong influence on contemporary fashions in architecture and applied art. New stylistic revivals arose, based on a combination of passionate Romanticism and antiquarian pre-occupations – Greek and Neoclassical; Romanesque and Gothic; Elizabethan and Jacobean. Many architects were inspired by continental precedents. Revivalist styles married archaeologically-derived detail with social requirements and aspirations of the day.

The origins of Gothic Revival in England and Wales lie in the eighteenth century. Its domination of British architecture during the nineteenth century was greatly influenced by the prolific architect and designer, Augustus Welby Northmore Pugin (1812–52), and his successors, such as the architect, William Butterfield (1814–1900), and the pre-Raphaelite architect-designer, William Burges (1827–81).

The Gothic Revival followed a number of principles, including fidelity to historical precedent, but did not create slavish copies of medieval form or methods. While the archaeological component was important, it was but one element and the end product was something new. The testing ground for modern medievalism was the Medieval Court of the International Exhibition of 1862, viewed by some critics as an apparent 'advance' backwards.

CAERPHILLY CASTLE.

Restored from a careful survey, by G. T. Clark

Engraving of Caerphilly Castle as it may have looked in the Middle Ages, possibly by a Mr Turnbull, published in 1850 by the ironmaster, engineer and antiquary George Thomas Clark (1809–98). It shows the inner and middle wards on the central island, built by Gilbert de Clare (d. 1295) mainly between 1268 and 1271. Interestingly the circular feature in the background known as the 'redoubt' is shown in the engraving to be contemporary with the castle, though Clark correctly believed that this was a later, Civil War, construction. Following some initial work by his father, the fourth marquis of Bute (1881–1947) restored Caerphilly Castle between 1928 and 1939. (Cambrian Archaeological Association)

Cardiff Castle is a spectacular example of architectural invention and fantasy in medieval and Italianate styles. This was William Burges's principal secular commission and he submitted a report on its redevelopment to the third marquis of Bute (1847–1900) in 1868. (Cadw)

WILLIAM BURGES AND CASTELL COCH

He inherited the plan; he invented the superstructure. Art has added an extra dimension to archaeology: debris translated into dreams.

J. Mordaunt Crook (from *William Burges and the High Victorian Dream*, 1981)

William Burges, described as the 'Lutyens of his generation', is renowned for his translation of High Gothic into the High Victorian vision of the Middle Ages. This is spectacularly illustrated by his restoration of the ruined thirteenth-century castle known as Castell Coch, just north of Cardiff. In 1871–72, he produced a scheme for the re-creation of the castle for the great Victorian Romantic and multi-millionaire, the third marquis of Bute (1847–1900). Work began in 1875, and the structure was completed by 1891.

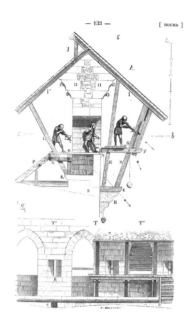

'Hourding', from Eugène-Emmanuel Viollet-le Duc's influential Dictionnaire Raisonné de l'Architecture Française du XIe au XVIe Siècle *(Paris, 1854–68, 10 vols). The arrangement originally proposed by Burges for the Well Tower at Castell Coch was similar. (National Museum of Wales)*

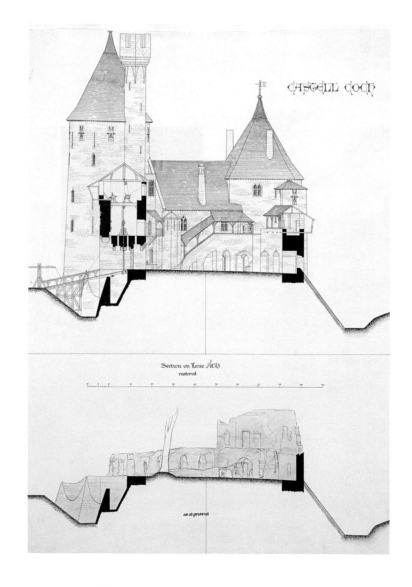

A page from The Castell Coch Report *by William Burges (fol. 24). The report, on the condition of the ruins of the medieval castle and proposals for its future (preservation or restoration), was submitted to the third marquis of Bute in 1872. The album contains many clever juxtapositions of the castle ruins and his proposals for their architectural reconstruction. His designs for the exterior reflect a remarkably accurate representation of a thirteenth-century castle in working order. Burges included archaeological information, much from work by G.T. Clark, copies of manuscript illustrations and comparisons with other castles in his report to justify his designs. The drawings were prepared by Burges on separate sheets of paper, which were then pasted into the folios of the report. (Cadw and National Museum of Wales)*

Like Burges, the marquis of Bute had a passion for archaeology and the medieval period, and was taken with Burges's scheme for full rebuilding. They became more partners than patron and architect, in a remarkable combination of wealth, skill and knowledge. Unlike the contemporary architect William Butterfield, who drew on English precedents for his designs, Burges turned to continental Europe for a rich source of inspiration, notably early French Gothic architecture. Burges's master plan was followed by successive architects after his death in 1881. Externally, the rebuilt castle reflects convincingly an authentic medieval fortification.

In his work, Burges sought out the finest craftsmen. Workshops of skilled masons were established in Cardiff mainly for the work on Cardiff Castle, but they continued when work on Castell Coch began. The leading Welsh sculptor Goscombe John (1860–1952) began his training in the workshops in Cardiff at the age of 14 as an apprentice woodcarver under his father, Thomas John.

The re-created Castell Coch (left) was imbued with great archaeological and historical awareness, influenced by the restoration of the French walled town of Carcassonne (Aude) by French architect, designer and writer Eugène-Emmanuel Viollet-le-Duc (1814–79), and Swiss castles at L'Aigle and Chillon on Lake Geneva (shown above). Burges made meticulous drawings of Chillon during his European travels. (Peter Humphries)

A mural from the banqueting hall of Castell Coch, by Horatio Walter Lonsdale (d. 1919). In a scene reminiscent of a medieval manuscript, a king directs the work of his master mason. (Cadw)

Working with Data

BREATHING LIFE INTO RAW DATA

It is interesting to note that in his discussion of the term 'antiquity', the French antiquary, Bernard de Montfaucon (1655–1741), recognized that illustration was integral to its study. Illustration is a powerful method of informing us about new discoveries and ideas concerning the past. Visual representations have always been influenced by factors such as the purpose of the illustration, its required content, contemporary conventions and the understanding and vision of the artist. For example, difficulties encountered in illustrating buildings accurately were eventually helped by the classification of different orders of architecture. Over the last 200 years, illustrating the past has changed with the dramatic development of archaeological techniques and the emergence of new scientific approaches. Romantic images of antiquity have been replaced by more accurate, academically tested versions. Just as the archaeologist in the field

Hunting and fishing about 8400 BC at The Nab Head, St Brides Bay, Pembrokeshire, by Giovanni Caselli (acrylic on plywood, 1979). The Nab Head is shown in the background, at a time when the sea level would have been lower than today, and the present headland would have been an inland hill. This illustration captures a range of Mesolithic activities on the coastal plain and incorporates evidence from a diverse range of sources, not all from Wales. It is unlikely that so many people would have been engaged simultaneously in all these activities: making a logboat with a chisel-shaped axe/adze, archery, making barbed antler points, smoking fish and meat over fires and fishing from boats. In many respects, it perpetuates traditional gender-specific ideas about early society.

14

now collaborates with a wide range of specialists who focus on particular fields of expertise, the re-creation process involves dialogue and collaboration between artist, archaeologist, conservator, craftsman, curator, anthropologist, forensic scientist and ecologist. Archaeologists have a responsibility to interpret the past and communicate their knowledge to a wide audience using the best techniques available. By their very nature, many visualizations are static interpretations and demonstrate differing levels of detail and sophistication. Nevertheless, the power of illustrations can remain long after the ideas they represent have become outmoded and their lifespan ended. As an alternative to the single authoritative view, the viewer may be invited to engage in an active process of interpretation and dialogue, by examining different versions based on the same archaeological data. Interpretations can remain fluid, reflecting the changing and transient nature of archaeological interpretation. At their best, re-creations stimulate further inquiry and debate – 'how do we know that?' – while others inspire or invoke caution, or invite comparison with today.

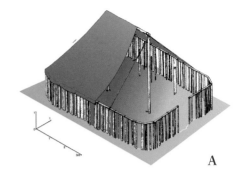

A

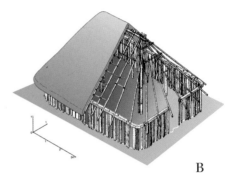

B

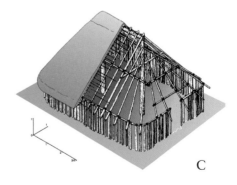

C

Maen Madoc, Ystradfellte, Powys. The son of Dervacus inspects his father's monument, by Alan Sorrell (crayon, ink and bodycolour, 1940). This sixth-century stone, which is inscribed in Latin 'Dervacus, son of Iustus' may be the site of a roadside burial. It was excavated by Sir Cyril and Lady Fox in 1940, and re-erected beside the Roman road between Neath and Brecon. Sorrell's picture draws upon the imagination, and engages the viewer in speculation and interpretation. The figures do not just provide scale – they are actors in a drama, and engaged in a visit to the memorial. Sorrell has used impressionistic rather than precise crayon work in the dress and bearing of the main character to suggest a continuity of Roman tradition in early medieval Wales.

Iron Age building, Goldcliff, Severn Estuary, tree-ring dated to about 273 BC. Sometimes different reconstructions based on the same data can be produced to accompany a discussion of their plausibility. (A) has a hide roof; (B) has composite axial posts and a squared wall plate; (C) has large axial posts, frames of roundwood posts and infilling of planks. (Drawing by S. J. Allen)

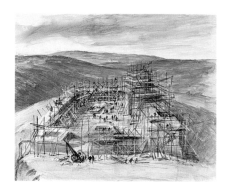

Carreg Cennen Castle, Carmarthenshire, under construction in the late thirteenth century, by Alan Sorrell (about 1960, watercolour and bodycolour over pencil, about 1960, preparatory sketch). The isolated castle is situated on a spectacular limestone crag above the Tywi Valley in the foothills of the Carmarthenshire Black Mountain. This small sketch gives an impression of the castle under construction, as the walls rise beneath a forest of wooden scaffolding. (National Museum of Wales)

THOUGHTS TRANSFORMED INTO IMAGE

People have never been able to live without art, and archaeology ... cannot be properly considered without it.

Alan Sorrell (from *The Artist and Reconstruction*, 1973)

The creative process of transforming archaeological data into a visual format is the result of careful planning, lengthy collaboration and close observation of detail. It often begins with a visit to the site by the artist and relevant specialists to settle the main points of detail. The skill of the illustrator lies in the ability to combine all the available data and to visualize in two or three dimensions. Reconstructions may be best guesses, but they have to be as accurate as possible, since they are often regarded by the public as 'official' interpretations. The 'realism' is often staged, with credible backdrops and accurate props, but the more detail a picture contains, the more speculation the image may incorporate.

Alan Sorrell (1904–74) dominated the field of reconstruction illustration during the post-War decades. He linked archaeology to humanistic culture, and his neo-Romantic style reflects the pre-Impressionist tradition of European visual art. For Sorrell, as for Zdenek Burian, the Czech painter of prehistoric people, the creative and the scientific existed symbiotically together. The description of Burian's work as 'novels with a scientific dimension' can also be applied to some of Sorrell's work. He viewed the present in terms of the past, and like painter/print-maker John Piper (1903–1992), saw continuities between prehistoric, medieval and modern worlds. His illustrations are full of atmosphere and eerie light effects, many characterized by dark rolling clouds, imminent rain and buffeting wind, piles of wood and mysterious darkness. Kenneth Clark (1903–83) once described some paintings and drawings as 'visual records pickled in style', in that they were only convincing when seen through a personality. Sorrell felt that the phrase could also be applied to reconstructions of archaeological subjects.

In 1936, his sketches of Kathleen Kenyon's excavations of the Roman forum at Leicester came to the attention of the *Illustrated London News*, which encouraged him to attempt a reconstruction of the *basilica*. Dr Mortimer Wheeler (1890–1976) commissioned similar reconstructions of Maiden Castle, Dorset, and Sir Cyril Fox (1882–1967) and Dr V. E. Nash-Williams (1897–1955) of the National Museum of Wales worked with Sorrell on a series of pictures of Roman Caerwent and Caerleon for gallery interpretation. After an interlude as Camouflage Officer during the Second World War, he resumed his connection with the National Museum of Wales in 1948. In the 1950s a series of reconstructions was commissioned by the then Ministry of Works (a predecessor of Cadw), beginning with drawings of castles at Conwy, Harlech and Beaumaris. Initially the Ancient Monuments Board discouraged the notion of speculation and such illustrations were reserved for postcards and on-site interpretation until the late 1960s, when they first appeared in 'blue' guides. As the nature of archaeology changed, by the early 1960s it was recognized that hypotheses needed to be published. This coincided with the growth of tourism and the need for visual interpretation. Sorrell's work later came in for some criticism because of the overuse of melodramatic settings and inaccurate scale, but it is the combination of his ability as a draughtsman with his imaginative style which make his work so attractive.

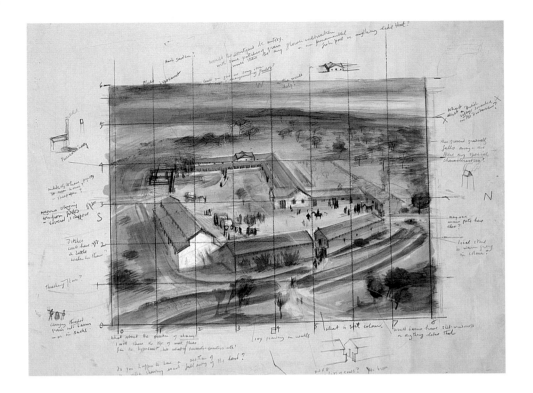

Llantwit Major Roman villa, Vale of Glamorgan, by Alan Sorrell (1949, watercolour, ink and pencil, squared up for transfer). This cartoon is annotated with points for clarification by the excavator, Dr V. E. Nash-Williams. It was produced in preparation for the final picture, after the last season of excavation, and was developed from maps, plans, photographs and sketches. (National Museum of Wales)

Sorrell's final version of Llantwit Major Roman villa (1949, bodycolour, ink and crayon). Dr Nash-Williams was of the opinion that the whole complex was built about AD 150. More recent excavations suggest that the villa, as shown, dates to the early fourth century AD, and that it had a stone and not a tiled roof. (National Museum of Wales)

Talley Abbey, Carmarthenshire, by Terry Ball (watercolour and ink over pencil, 1998). The abbey was founded by Rhys ap Gruffudd (d. 1197), prince of Deheubarth, for the Premonstratensian or 'White' canons. The proposed abbey and what was actually built are shown in this ghosting sequence related to the wall footings which remain today. Detailed study of the surviving masonry and foundation footings provided sufficient clues for this unusual reconstruction. (Cadw)

Since the death of Alan Sorrell, a number of artists have emerged in the field of archaeological reconstruction, such as Terry Ball (b. 1931), who went to the local art school in Sutton, Surrey, at the age of 15, and later studied painting at the Royal College of Art. In 1957 he worked as a draftsman on Kathleen Kenyon's final season of excavation at Jericho, illustrating objects from tombs. This was followed by ten years of work in Palestine and Jerusalem. After the turbulent events of 1967 in the Middle East, he moved to the suburbs of London and started surveying and preparing measured drawings for the Ministry of Public Building and Works, later English Heritage. His first reconstruction drawing for Cadw: Welsh Historic Monuments was of Conwy Castle, published in their 1985 guidebook (replacing the Sorrell version), and this led to further commissions. A benefit of working closely with Cadw, English Heritage and the earlier Ministry of Public Building and Works was that all the archives, plans and photographs of particular sites could be studied in close collaboration with archaeologists and architects. This research would be followed by site visits and making sketches which would then be worked up, possibly with additional photography. He constructs models of the more complex sites in order to get a sense of depth and to work out the best angle from which to make a drawing: 'a photograph cannot describe something in the way that a drawing can. Drawing, like writing, is a selective process. The final view would be chosen for the amount of information conveyed ('how did it work?'), rather than its dramatic effect. But I could not be unaware of the romantic and topographic painters and illustrators who have been big influences on my work – from traditional French architects such as Viollet-le-Duc and watercolour artists such as Thomas Girtin (1775–1802) onwards.'

Ivan Lapper (b. 1939) started to illustrate at the age of twelve on a one-day-a-week day release from school to Bilston Art College. After studying at Wolverhampton College of Art, in 1959 he moved to the Royal College of Art, where he studied illustration, painting and drawing for three years. He has been a freelance illustrator since 1962, on a wide range of subjects for books, newspapers and advertising, and he covered the Aberfan disaster for *The Daily Express* in 1966. In the 1980s he was asked by the Education Department of English Heritage to illustrate a castle for on-site interpretation, and further work followed. Like Terry Ball, he often prepares by making a scale model of his subject out of a range of materials. The models, whether of buildings, interiors or panoramic views, enable him to work out exactly how something would have worked, and to select the best possible viewpoint. He normally paints from a digital photograph of the finished model, and then adds the detail. Influences on his work have been David Stone Martin, Titian figure drawing and Stanley Spencer: 'as a figure artist, not an architect, I have tried to introduce more atmosphere into the paintings, and put more emphasis on showing how the people of the time lived.'

A rough model of Kidwelly Castle and town, Carmarthenshire, in the early fifteenth century. It was made by Ivan Lapper in order to devise a justifiable solution to every detail prior to drafting an illustration. Photographs of the model became the basis for perspective views. (Ivan Lapper, 2001)

The style adopted by Dylan Roberts (b. 1941), while working for the Royal Commission on the Ancient and Historical Monuments of Wales evolved from figurative painting, and was particularly influenced by Alan Sorrell. For the illustration of Coity Castle, he was on site with Jack Spurgeon and Howard Thomas for five weeks, making plans, sections and elevations. Chris Jones-Jenkins (b. 1954) studied at the Welsh School of Architecture (1973–77). Having decided not to become an architect, he worked at the Welsh Folk Museum (now Museum of Welsh Life), St Fagans, on analytical drawings and surveys of buildings that were being reconstructed. Since 1984, he has worked as a freelance illustrator for Cadw: Welsh Historic Monuments. Illustration is a part-time interest, since he now works for the Vale of Glamorgan Council. Most of his reconstructions are destined for Cadw guidebooks or on-site interpretation panels. The first stage may be a site visit with specialists from Cadw, when he will take measurements and photographs. His architectural background is evident in the surveyed approach to his drawings, which are usually concerned with the architectural reconstruction of castles and abbeys. Rough versions are discussed and altered, often undergoing a prolonged process of modification. Artwork is usually in pen and ink on transparent film. Reduced copies on A3 watercolour cartridge paper may be produced to have colour added.

Each reconstruction picture is the result of careful planning and close observation of detail. Unlike the illustration of fiction, the images are not invented compositions, but the products of a series of decisions made by artists in conjunction with archaeologists and other specialists. For most illustrators, atmosphere is secondary to presenting the evidence as accurately as possible. Where direct evidence is absent, information from elsewhere is researched in order to find solutions which appear to fit the available evidence. According to Mark Hassall, 'If it doesn't work, it can't be right, but if it works, it may be right, and that is real progress'. In this way, attempts to re-create the most likely forms of missing elements of a site frequently contribute to archaeological interpretation as well as public appreciation.

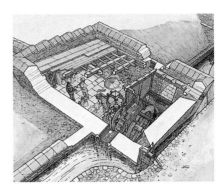

Caerphilly Castle medieval mill, Caerphilly, by Chris Jones-Jenkins (watercolour and ink, 1989, with modifications 1997). The mill was in operation from the thirteenth to the seventeenth centuries. This cutaway reconstruction shows the arrangements by which the overshot wheel, which powers the mill, was driven. Cutaway drawings can provide clear visual interpretations of complex structures and mechanisms. This illustration was the result of extensive research on the surviving structure, and drew upon comparative material and advice from specialists on mills. (Cadw)

Coity Castle, Bridgend, by Dylan Roberts, as it may have looked following the sixteenth-century refurbishment (1990; pencil, ink and charcoal; Crown copyright, RCAHMW)

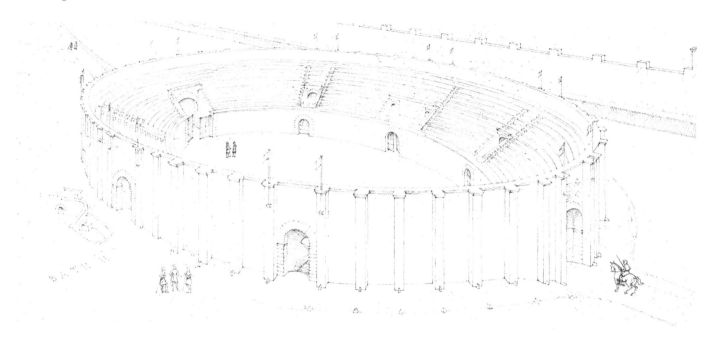

Roman amphitheatre, Caerleon, by J. A. Wright (pencil, 1928). Wright shows the amphitheatre, excavated in 1926–27, outside the fortress of the Second Augustan Legion in the late first century AD. Mortimer Wheeler, Director of the National Museum of Wales from 1924–26, capitalized on local tradition which knew the site as 'Arthur's Round Table'. Excavation of the amphitheatre was funded by sponsorship from the Daily Mail (supervised by Tessa Wheeler and Nowell Myres). At the time it was thought that the auditorium was supported by a bank of earth retained by masonry walls. The original height was determined from the remains of arches and vaulting in the main entrances. Wright, who worked for the Office of Works (a predecessor of Cadw), was responsible for producing the plans and sections of the excavations, as well as for an appendix on the Roman planning and setting out of the amphitheatre in the report published in the journal Archaeologia, 1928. (National Museum of Wales)

Roman amphitheatre, Caerleon, by Alan Sorrell (acrylic, 1939). Between 1937 and 1940, Sorrell worked in close collaboration with the National Museum of Wales on a series of archaeological reconstructions, and for the first time, archaeology dominated his artistic output. This view borrows from the reconstruction by Wright, but shows more activity and detail in the vicinity of the amphitheatre. (National Museum of Wales)

Roman amphitheatre, Caerleon, by John Banbury (bodycolour, pencil, crayon, watercolour and ink, 1988). This reconstruction also shows the amphitheatre as it may have looked in the late first century AD. John Banbury (1938–1997), who was born in Cardiff and studied commercial art and graphic design at Swansea College of Art, based this reconstruction on a drawing by Robert Anderson (1981), produced in collaboration with the late George Boon and Richard Brewer. Anderson, a draughtsman with the Department of the Environment, used the same perspective as the Wright drawing of 1920, but included the results of the new discoveries from the 1962 excavations; the upper tiers of seating are shown supported by a timber framework, rather than carried to full height in masonry. (Cadw)

Caernarfon Castle, Gwynedd, under attack by Madog ap Llywelyn's force in September 1294, by Ivan Lapper (acrylic, pencil and crayon, 1993). This imaginative reconstruction of a historic event uses information from a range of sources to build up an impression of the Welsh assault. At the time of the attack, building work on the castle within the confines of the town had not progressed far, enabling the Welsh to burn the castle's timber buildings and lay waste the town. (Cadw)

Criccieth Castle, Gwynedd, about 1240, by Ivan Lapper (acrylic, pencil and crayon, 1988). The dating of the surviving structural remains is controversial and has undergone several revisions. This picture, reflecting the current interpretation, shows the inner ward built by Llywelyn ab Iorwerth some time between 1230 and his death in 1240. Modern interpretations of such building histories may also be subject to revision as a result of further research. (Cadw)

The Bishop's Palace, St Davids, Pembrokeshire, about 1530, by Alan Sorrell (watercolour, crayon, pencil and ink, 1958). Built mainly on the instruction of Bishop Henry de Gower (1328–47), the Bishop's Palace stands in the cathedral close. Tradition associates the cathedral area with the site of David's monastic foundation in the sixth century. Sorrell has focused on the range of buildings and courtyard, with the great hall to the left. (Cadw)

The great hall of the Bishop's Palace, St Davids, Pembrokeshire, about 1350, by Terry Ball (watercolour and bodycolour over pencil, 1991, modified 1999). This cutaway of the imposing hall, built in the Decorated style of medieval Gothic architecture, shows the position of a wooden screen to hide servants approaching from the kitchen, or the undercrofts below the hall. The bishop and his guests are shown at the high table at the far end of the hall. The illustration is based on new architectural analysis, and close examination of the surviving structure has allowed a putative reconstruction of the massive trussed roof, now missing. (Cadw)

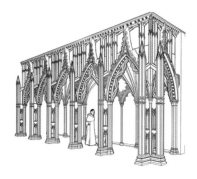

The pulpitum, Tintern Abbey, Monmouthshire, about 1325–30, by Chris Jones-Jenkins (ink on permatrace, copied onto paper, 1997). (Cadw)

REASSEMBLING THE PAST

It is sometimes surprising how far one can go in reconstructing what no longer survives. Essential to accurate reconstruction is scholarly research and collaboration between specialists, whose investigations may lead far beyond previously explored boundaries to provoke questions not asked before. In some cases reconstruction projects may even launch a major programme of academic research.

Tintern Abbey, Monmouthshire, was founded in 1131, and was the second monastery of the Cistercian order to be established in Britain. The abbey church was largely rebuilt between 1269 and 1301, and fitting out continued after this date. Cadw brought together a team of experts to investigate the scattered collections of loose stonework at the abbey in order to reconstruct the fourteenth-century pulpitum – the decorative stone screen between nave and choir. Specialists collaborated over several years to identify the form of the screen (Stuart M. Harrison), its dating and attribution (Richard K. Morris) and its archaeological and historical context (David M. Robinson). The form of the reconstruction was the result of careful recording of all the moulded profiles, coupled with extensive comparative research. The fragments were then painstakingly pieced together like a massive jigsaw puzzle, and drawn by reconstruction artist Chris Jones-Jenkins.

Cutaway reconstruction of the abbey church at Tintern, by Terry Ball (watercolour, 2002). The picture shows the internal liturgical arrangements and decoration about 1330; the form of the flèche (spire) over the crossing and of the porch outside the west door are conjectural. (Cadw)

SETTING THE SCENE

Soil, vegetation and fauna are no mere background to human cultures, but the very seed-bed in which they grow.

Grahame Clark (from *Archaeology and Society*, 1960)

Prehistoric hunting scene about 250,000 BC, by Gino D'Achille (about 1980), showing Penarth Head, Cardiff (on left), Flat Holm and Somerset in the background. The vegetation, fauna and low sea level contrast dramatically with the same scene today. (National Museum of Wales)

Our past is not just based on the physical remains of buildings and artefacts. Reconstructions can be used to place people, objects and sites within their environmental and geographic contexts. Climate, soils, vegetation, habitats and all forms of life have defined the opportunities for particular ways of life and the context for human actions. The landscape is rarely constant, and is subject to seasonal and long-term changes, some of which are climatic, others being induced by people.

The enhanced recovery of data provides growing opportunities for reconstructing former environments and assessing the human impact on them through time. Flotation, a process of sieving soil samples using running water, will recover seeds

Harlech Castle, Gwynedd, by Alan Sorrell (1957), in a medieval landscape, when it was probably supplied by ship. Today the castle is landlocked, the sea having receded over a kilometre since the Middle Ages. (Cadw)

providing information on crops and other plants, as well as small rodent and fish bones. Animal bones survive well in calcareous soils, while pollen from more acid soils can be identified and used to indicate past vegetation – whether woodland, grassland, scrub or meadow. The potential for researching early agriculture in different bio-climatic zones has been exemplified at Butser Ancient Farm, Hampshire, where fields, stock areas, animal paddocks, and livestock were maintained: five breeds of sheep, Old English goats, Dexter cattle, Old English Game fowl, and occasionally Tamworth or European Wild boar. Established by Peter Reynolds (1939–2001) in 1972 as a centre for research and education, its original aim was to study the agricultural and domestic economy of the Iron Age, covering the period from about 400 BC to AD 400. Work at this and subsequent sites has revolutionized ideas about prehistoric agriculture in temperate Europe.

The past appearance of natural features such as hills, valleys, floodplains, rivers and streams are important aspects of archaeological reconstruction. Fields may have had crops, animals or natural vegetation. By combining evidence from documents and maps, the analysis of evidence of field boundaries using aerial photography and excavation evidence, illustrators can convert diagrams and other 'dry' data into a vivid portrayal of ancient landscapes.

Laugharne Castle and town, Carmarthenshire, in the mid-fourteenth century, by Ivan Lapper (1994). The coastal stronghold at the mouth of the River Taf is shown as it may have appeared prior to modernization by Guy de Brian VII (d. 1390). The eye-level view engages the observer with activity in the foreground. (Cadw)

Interpreting in Three Dimensions

ARTEFACTS

Archaeology is digging up, not things, but people.

Sir Mortimer Wheeler (from *Archaeology from the Earth*, 1954)

Displayed objects often do not communicate directly with observers. For their messages to be understood, artefacts have to be interpreted. Common questions are: What is it? What did it originally look like? How did it work? How was it made? What is it made of? How significant is it? Reconstructions of their original appearance are attractive interpretative tools. The final step is to learn from the artefacts about the people who made or used them.

Research on all aspects from the processing of raw materials, the fabrication and decoration of the artefacts, to their use, reuse and discard, can provide answers to key questions. Replicas are often used to illustrate what objects originally looked like and to explore the technology of their manufacture. This may also involve experimental archaeology in trying to re-create lost production processes.

FIREDOGS AND SMITHS

In 1852 an Iron Age firedog with 'ox-head' terminals was found on its side, with a large stone at each end, in a peat bog at Capel Garmon, Llanrwst, Gwynedd. The wrought-iron firedog may have been the work of a north Wales blacksmith attached to the house of a chieftain (the patron) during the early first century AD. Firedogs, used in pairs, stood by the hearth in the centre of a roundhouse. The object conveyed many messages. The terminal designs marry the power of horned ox heads with horses manes, and provide us with one of the finest iron objects in European Iron Age art. The form and elaboration symbolize the wealth and authority of the patron, and the importance of the feast. Such items were highly valued, and were often chosen to accompany their owners to the grave.

Mild steel replicas of the Capel Garmon firedogs were made by the artist-blacksmith David Petersen in 1991, for display in a reconstructed roundhouse. Following X-radiography of the original object which revealed new details of its construction, a total of 85 separate pieces of iron were made and assembled (including 30 rivets and 34 applied heads). Its construction relies on riveting and demonstrates a mastery of ironworking technology.

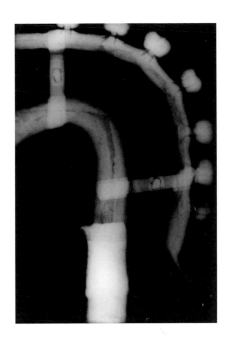

X-radiograph of the original Capel Garmon firedog showing the mane, into which 7 rivets, each with separately applied heads, have been inserted. This technique was replicated on the copy. (National Museum of Wales)

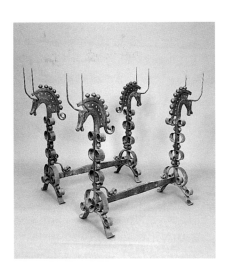

The replica Capel Garmon firedogs. (National Museum of Wales)

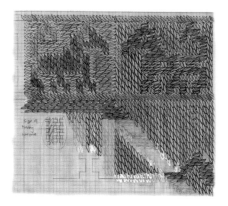

Diagram of stitches for a border motif on the embroidered textile from Llan-gors crannog, Powys, by Louise Mumford (2002). (National Museum of Wales)

CLOTHING A ROYAL DYNASTY

Charred fragments of embroidered linen were discovered in 1990 during excavation of the early medieval crannog on Llan-gors Lake, Powys. This royal residence of the rulers of the kingdom of Brycheiniog was constructed between AD 889 and 893, and destroyed by a Mercian (Saxon) army in AD 916.

The textile was found as a waterlogged lump made up of many layers. Conservation staff carefully separated and cleaned the fragments, and allowed them to dry. Some of the fragments of linen proved to have silk embroidery. Although the bright colours are now blackened, and the fabric is worn and decayed, parts of the design have been deciphered in a painstaking process of stitch by stitch recording. This involved tracing threads from enlarged photographs in conjunction with microscopic examination of the textile. Acetate tracings were then assembled and redrawn.

The Llan-gors textile combines exceptional needlework skills with a familiarity with exotic silk designs, compatible with royal ownership. The embroidery and constructional sewing were carried out in the same place, somewhere in Britain; whether the garment, which had a belt loop, was made locally in Wales or brought from England, only further research will unravel.

Digitized photographs of motifs on the textile from Llan-gors crannog, suggesting possible colours obtained from natural dyes. The original colour scheme is not known, but the use of colour on contemporary textiles provides clues. (National Museum of Wales)

Reconstruction of the embroidered design, which is made up of stylized vine scrolls, with leaves and bunches of grapes, which contain various birds (Tony Daly, 2001). The edges of the panels have borders containing pairs of lions or geometric designs, and the seams are covered with tiny silk braids. Such motifs may be derived from those common on woven silks of the same period from Central Asia. (National Museum of Wales)

CHARIOTS

Scale models can effectively help us understand complex structures. For example, the two models illustrated provide alternative interpretations of a later Iron Age chariot (about 50 BC – AD 50), and are based on the fittings from the lake-edge metalwork deposit found at Llyn Cerrig Bach, Isle of Anglesey. A third possibility exists, for the finds of iron tyres from the deposit represent at least ten vehicles, some perhaps from four-wheeled wagons or two-wheeled carts rather than chariots. Britons of the Iron Age have long been associated with chariots – vehicles of prestige and status symbols, combining strength with lightness. Classical sources describe them carrying both charioteer and rider, as depicted on coins of the period. They were pulled by small horses the size of ponies.

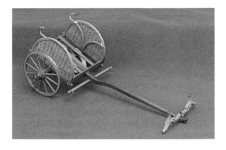

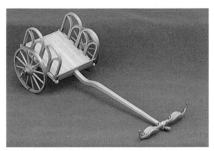

The earlier model (top, made by Mr H. R. Waiting, 1946) was based on the interpretation by Sir Cyril Fox (Director of the Museum 1926–48), which incorporated evidence from the Continent. It has a pair of chariot horns as hand-grips for mounting the chariot, semi-circular basketwork side-screens and a two-terret (harness-ring) array on the yoke. The later model (bottom, made by Mr C. Williams, 1978) is a revision produced in the light of additional chariot depictions and new research. Dr H. N. Savory (Keeper of Archaeology 1955–76) always believed that it had side-screens in the form of pairs of open hoops, based on images of chariots on coins of the first century BC and a relief from Padua. The horn caps are now shown fitted to the yoke tips, and there is a four-terret array along the yoke. (National Museum of Wales)

Recent research has suggested that the Iron Age chariot may have had suspension. The open hoops could have supported a series of leather thongs which carried a floor made from a web of rawhide straps. This full-size reconstruction by Robert Hurford, commissioned for the BBC programme Meet the Ancestors, *is based on a fourth-century BC chariot burial at Wetwang, Yorkshire. (British Museum)*

Penmaen, Castle Tower, Gower, as it might have appeared in the twelfth or early thirteenth centuries. This small-scale diorama (made by Roy Herbert, about 1968) incorporates the evidence from excavations in 1960–61 with a reconstruction of what the ringwork may have looked like by Alan Sorrell. Some of the archaeological detail shown is now known to be incorrect. (National Museum of Wales)

DIORAMAS

During the later nineteenth century, museums responded to the growth of knowledge about the past by creating displays of life-size habitat dioramas and life-group displays. Those at the *Exposition Universelle* in Paris of 1889 *(L'Histoire de l'Habitation, L'Histoire du travail)* illustrated the manual, material and intellectual progress of humanity through time, a persistent theme during this period.

The small-scale diorama of Penmaen, Castle Tower, is one of a series of dioramas based on sites in Wales from the Palaeolithic to late medieval periods. They were created for the new archaeology galleries at the National Museum of Wales which were opened in stages from 1965. Local artist, Arthur Miles, painted the backgrounds of the earlier dioramas onto the curved backboards. The foregrounds were modelled by Harry Gear, technician in the Department of Archaeology. Later dioramas were modelled by Roy Herbert, maker of wax models in the Department of Botany.

Penmaen, Castle Tower, Gower, by Terry Ball (1987). This general view illustrates an attack on the ringwork, during which the phase I gate-tower was destroyed by fire. The castle was destroyed by the Welsh prince, Rhys Gryg (d. 1233), ally of Llywelyn ab Iorwerth, in 1217. Terry Ball has always been particularly excited by the landscape and physical setting of the sites on the Gower. This reconstruction differs from the 1960s diorama, incorporating new evidence from other sites about the likely appearance of the rampart and the layout of the interior, crowded with timber buildings with steep roof pitches. (Cadw)

BOAT TIMBERS AND FULL-SIZE MODELS

Sometimes the shape of discoveries can only be determined satisfactorily by re-creating the design and construction process.

In 1994 the remains of a large boat, constructed about AD 1241, were excavated and recovered from the intertidal muds of the Severn Estuary, near Magor Pill. Following the recording of the boat timbers, a full-size model of the surviving hull structure was commissioned by the National Museums & Galleries of Wales in order to determine the most likely shape and form of the original vessel.

Defining the main elements and overall dimensions from incomplete, fractured and distorted timbers resembled a three-dimensional jigsaw with many parts missing. The form of such a vessel is, in part, determined by the way in which the planks respond to shaping by the carpenter. This was part of the 'design' process of the original boat which can best be replicated with a large model. Full-size modelling supported by tracings of the original timbers offered the most accurate solution to the correct positioning of fastenings and timbers. The model has provided a template for the conservation of the original timbers and an aid for their future re-assembly.

The reconstruction showed that the original craft was a double-ended boat with good stability and load-carrying capabilities. Under sail the boat originally had a minimum length of 13.2m and a single, square-sail rig. It would have been capable of coastal and even sea voyages, at speeds of about six to seven knots in a moderate breeze. The surviving cargo on board the boat was high-grade iron ore, probably from Glamorgan (the Miskin/Llantrisant area), in both powder and lump form.

The Magor Pill boat during excavation in 1994. (National Museum of Wales)

The full-size model of the Magor Pill boat, constructed by E. W. H. Gifford and craftsmen at Griffon Hovercraft Ltd, Southampton. (National Museum of Wales)

An early fifteenth-century archer, by the David Hayes Studio (2002). The clothes were made by Jane Cowood. The arrows have mild steel 'bodkin' heads replicating examples found at Criccieth Castle, Gwynedd. The replica longbow has a linen drawstring and is based on examples shown in manuscript sources and those recovered from the wreck of the Mary Rose (1545). Much of the equipment is based on objects in the museum collections, such as the early fifteenth-century rondel dagger (based on an example found about 1880 close to Dolwyddelan Castle, Conwy), and was made by the White Rose Armoury & Heritage Arms, Hector Cole Ironwork and Bickerstaffe Bows. (National Museum of Wales)

ARTEFACTS IN CONTEXT

For the garniture of the castle at Kidwelly … We order that … you buy six habergeons, six basinets, six visors, six pairs of vambraces, six pairs of gauntlets, six jacks, 12 lances, six poleaxes, 40 bows, 12 dozen arrows for the bows, 80 bushels of arrows … 18 cords for the crossbowmen, six crossbows, a windlass, a pulley for the crossbows…

From an order for arms and armour to be sent to Kidwelly Castle, dated 30 November 1405, during the Owain Glyn Dŵr rebellion (Public Record Office DL42/15 fol. 177)

The open-face basinet helmet is based on contemporary examples and has been made with the same range of tools found in a medieval workshop. The completed arrow shafts have horn knocks, and are fletched with goose feather. (National Museum of Wales)

Our past is a story of individuals, and we relate most easily to other people. Models provide a means of bridging the gap between artefacts and people's lives, by providing a human context for objects otherwise displayed in isolation. Creating any figure from the past requires extensive research. For example, what sort of sandals would a Roman legionary soldier have worn at Caerleon? Would an early fifteenth-century Welsh archer have had a long or short bow? Many such details have to be resolved before a figure can be made.

The figure shown opposite represents a Welsh archer from the time of Owain Glyn Dŵr (about 1359–1415), self-styled prince of Wales, who led a rebellion against the English Crown which lasted from 1400 to about 1410. The correct stance for the figure was provided by a longbow specialist, who was photographed and measured. The finished model is clothed with a linen shirt under a short-sleeved padded jack (a quilted cloth protective jacket) of natural wool. The livery coat in green and white wool is similar to that bought to make jackets and hoods for Welsh bowmen of *Flynt* in the service of Edward, The Black Prince, in 1346. On his legs he wears hose in a light wool, coloured dark red with natural dye (madder), and over this another separate pair of leggings which could be rolled down to the ankles (dark brown/grey wool). He also wears a linen coif (or head-dress) under his helmet, a woollen hood on his shoulders and a pair of one-piece leather ankle boots.

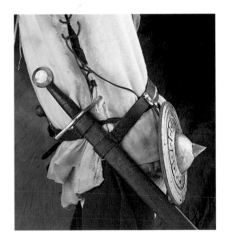

The sword is based on a fourteenth-century example found in the 'moat or ditch' at Cardiff Castle. The buckler (small shield) is a copy of one lost in London in the 1380s. Ruabon and Wrexham were the main centres for buckler-making in the fifteenth and sixteenth centuries, and numerous metaphors were used by the Welsh poets to describe their products: ' a picture of the sun full of rivets', a 'steel moon', 'planets in steel honeycombs', 'a steel cloister, a good court for the fist'. (National Museum of Wales)

Left: *Medieval siege of a well-defended castle, from* The Thebais of Statius, *France, about 1400. No weapon was so feared by enemies as the longbow. An archer's training from an early age meant that with considerable physical skill and mental control he could draw weights of between 44kg and 83kg, and shoot accurately with a range of at least 262m. (London, British Library, Burney MS 257 fol. 168)*

The influential reconstruction of the rampart and eastern gateway at the Lunt Roman Fort, Baginton (showing the Royal Engineers constructing the eastern gateway in 1970). Many of the first-century forts in Wales would have looked similar.

Firing an Iron Age furnace at the Museum of Welsh Life in 1998. Each day-long smelt requires the work of three people and consumes up to 30kg of iron ore and 100kg of charcoal to produce one iron bloom (lump of slaggy iron) weighing up to 7kg, from which smaller billets of iron could be wrought. Similar experiments on the technology of early iron making have taken place at Plas Tan y Bwlch, Snowdonia National Park Study Centre, Maentwrog.

EXPERIMENTS IN CONSTRUCTION: LEARNING THE HARD WAY

It represents no more and no less than a channelling of intelligent curiosity towards an exploration of human behaviour in essentially practical terms.

J. Coles (from *Archaeology by Experiment,* 1973)

There are many questions about the past that we cannot yet answer. Experimental archaeology aims to test different hypotheses that are based on archaeological evidence. By simulating what may have happened and by investigating the effect of different variables, it seeks to close the gap between available data and what may have happened. An impressive form of experimental archaeology, when underpinned by academic and scientific research, is the full-scale re-creation of buildings, earthworks, boats and siege engines. Other trials include the uses of pottery, the firing of kilns, the fabrication and use of artefacts, the re-creation of what people ate and how they cooked, and their ancient cosmetics and medicines.

An early experimenter was Colonel Augustus Henry Lane Fox (later known as General Pitt-Rivers, 1827–1900). He commissioned copies of prehistoric tools recovered from flint mines that he was excavating in 1876, as well as models in wood or wire and plaster of sites such as the prehistoric burial chamber at Pentre Ifan, Pembrokeshire. An early German pioneer was Major E. Schramm, who in 1904 demonstrated replicas of Roman artillery to Kaiser Wilhelm II.

Reconstruction, however, may be limited to the restoration of surviving monuments, such as the rebuilding of much of Hadrian's Wall by John Clayton in the 1830s–50s, and the re-erection of the western arc of stones forming the great Bronze Age circle at Avebury, by Alexander Keiller in the 1930s. Alternatively, methods of construction may be tested. In 1954 Paul Johnson and the BBC recorded the transportation of a concrete replica of a Stonehenge bluestone by boats along the river Avon and by sledge on land to test the hypothesis that they could have been moved from the Preseli range in north Pembrokeshire by people.

Some experiments may be long term, and the reconstructions may be called 'imaginative constructs' or 'simulations'. Recording and understanding the weathering of earthworks is the goal of an experiment which began at Overton Down, Wiltshire, in 1960. The pioneering experimental reconstruction of a section of Roman timber and turf rampart at the Lunt Roman Fort, Baginton (1966) investigated both construction technique and subsequent weathering, on the original site. Simulations of its timber eastern gateway (1970), a granary and circular arena known as the 'gyrus' (1973), give a vivid impression of the type of fort constructed at the time of the Roman conquest of Wales in the first century AD.

Open-air museums with collections of buildings illustrating rural life originated in late nineteenth-century Scandinavia. The Museum of Welsh Life opened in 1948, and since then has established itself as one of Europe's finest open-air museums, in the grounds of St Fagans Castle, just outside Cardiff. Its primary purpose is the illustration and interpretation of the daily life and work of the people of Wales from the Middle Ages to the present. Historic buildings, rescued from decay or demolition are rebuilt in the grounds, and form an important part of its collections. One of the first buildings to be rebuilt in the early 1950s was a timber-framed cruck barn, tree-ring dated to about 1550. While the medieval and later structures have been carefully restored to their former states, some open-air exhibits are full-scale three-dimensional 'simulations' of earlier structures, based on archaeological evidence. In 1992, a simulation of an Iron Age settlement was completed, and the chronological range of the 'time-capsules' was later extended to the Early Bronze Age with the re-creation of a 'Stonehenge-style' timber circle, based on the 1990–91 excavations of the timber circle at Sarn-y-bryn-caled, near Welshpool, Powys (dated about 2100 BC).

The 1980s and 1990s witnessed renewed interest in re-creating sites of different periods and types. An Iron Age settlement has been reconstructed at Castell Henllys hillfort, north Pembrokeshire, excavated by the University of York. On this site, roundhouses have been re-created in their original positions within the remains of an inland promontory fort. Being on the actual site ('in situ', as at the Lunt Roman Fort), the simulations have been more potent in bringing visitors closer to the past. The Jorvik Viking Centre at York, opened in 1984 (and revised in 2001), revolutionized the interpretation of archaeological sites by combining reconstructions of excavated buildings from tenth-century York in tableaux with displays on the archaeological evidence. Such constructions can bring both formal and informal learning benefits, particularly when visitors are engaged in the interpretation process on the site and interactive participation through interpreters.

These thirteenth- and fourteenth-century buildings at Cosmeston near Penarth, Vale of Glamorgan, have been reconstructed 'in situ', following excavation of the medieval village, started in 1977 by the Glamorgan-Gwent Archaeological Trust. The site, which now forms part of Cosmeston Lakes Country Park, is managed by the local authority and interprets medieval life, with the assistance of living-history facilitators. (Glamorgan-Gwent Archaeological Trust Ltd)

ENGINES OF WAR

In 1991, Cadw commissioned the research, design and construction of four replica medieval engines of war – a *ballista* (a great crossbow), a *mangonel* (a catapult with a throwing arm powered by a large skein of twisted rope, sinew or hair), a *perrier* (a lever-operated stone-throwing catapult powered by a team of men hauling down on ropes) and a *trébuchet* (a large lever-operated catapult, the most effective of the siege engines, powered by the weight of a stone-filled box). These replicas, now on display at Caerphilly Castle, were built at full size and in full operational order, and have been used at regular demonstrations. Their range depends on the weight of the missile (stone balls weighing around 25kg have been found in Wales) and the degree of power applied. In tests at Caerphilly, the perrier powered by 6

The replica siege engines, with trébuchet in foreground, being demonstrated at Caerphilly Castle. (Cadw)

men hurled a 5kg stone ball 110m, and the mangonel hurled a 4kg stone 80m, whilst the trébuchet propelled much larger ammunition of 15kg or more for a distance of 120m. Siege engines like these were in common use throughout the medieval period, and their effectiveness is often vividly described in medieval accounts: both Dolforwyn Castle (Powys) and Dryslwyn Castle (Carmarthenshire) fell to bombardment by trébuchet in the late thirteenth century, whilst at Harlech Castle piles of stone ammunition have been found.

AN IRON AGE VILLAGE

Dr Peter Reynolds at work on the roof of a roundhouse

In 1992 the Museum of Welsh Life commissioned Dr Peter Reynolds of Butser Ancient Farm to re-create a 'Celtic' Iron Age village. A stockaded bank and ditch surrounding the village, a four-post granary, a tall rack or frame for drying fodder and a timber gateway were built. Three roundhouses were re-created to represent those found in Britain. They were based on the excavated plans of a stake-walled house from Moel y Gaer hillfort, Rhosesmor, Flintshire (excavated 1972–74), a stone-walled roundhouse from Conderton Camp, Worcestershire (excavated 1958–59) and a large post-ring roundhouse from Moel y Gerddi, near Harlech, Gwynedd (excavated 1980–81). When populated with re-enactors, it provides a vivid simulation of life 2,000 years ago.

The completed Iron Age village at the Museum of Welsh Life.

A CHURCH BEFORE THE REFORMATION

The re-erection and refurbishment of the medieval church of St Teilo from Llandeilo Tal-y-bont, Pontarddulais, near Swansea, is one of the Museum of Welsh Life's most ambitious projects. The church was abandoned in about 1970 and offered to the museum in 1984. A year later, the careful process of dismantling the structure began. This above-ground archaeology revealed, amongst other things, two important series of pre-Reformation wall-paintings, which were recorded and conserved. The entire church was repainted about 1500 with scenes from the life of Christ. It was decided to rebuild and refurbish the church as it would have appeared about 1520, using architectural clues recorded during the dismantling process and the results of an archaeological excavation which recorded the wall foundations.

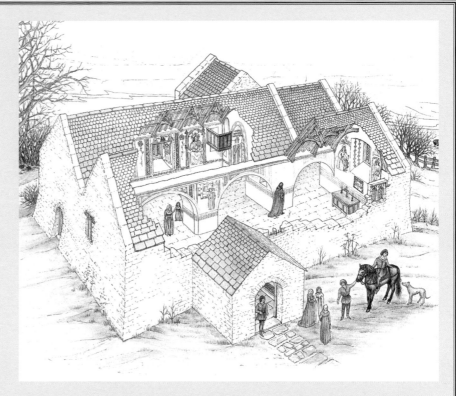

The medieval church, as it may have appeared about 1520, by Jane Durrant (watercolour, about 1992), who worked on the site before it was dismantled: 'a drawing must have a heart, and knowing the site intimately helps achieve this'. (National Museum of Wales)

Above and right: *Reconstruction of the church in progress in 2002. (National Museum of Wales)*

Looking at People

DEATH HAS THE LAST WORD

Mortal remains may be compared with books in a library of past lives, from which many personal histories may be read. They provide the raw material for the study of past societies, social hierarchy, environment, family, health, hygiene, diet, burial customs and occupations.

Disturbing a grave is never undertaken lightly. Bodies are examined under Home Office licence, with care and respect. Detailed records will be made of the position of the skeleton and its context. Experts will study the remains to determine the age at death, sex, stature, robustness, physique and health of the individual. Forensic anthropology will try to identify an individual and the manner of death, any deviation from normal appearance and the presence of injuries.

Advances in scientific techniques, in studies of the human genome and palaeopathology are continually extending what we know about our ancestors and where they came from. Sympathetically interpreted, human remains can provide clues which enable specialists to re-create details of past lives, and the worlds they once inhabited.

Tinkinswood Neolithic chambered tomb, St Nicholas, Vale of Glamorgan, by Alan Sorrell (gouache/bodycolour and ink on paper, 1940), based on excavations by John Ward in 1914. This image from about 4000–3500 BC focuses on the human story, and re-creates a burial ceremony which involved the local community and ritual sacrifice. Sorrell's rigorous preparation for the picture started with a visit to the site, his most important source of information, where he would try to 'get into the minds of the old builders, and savour something of their problems and achievements.'

PAST LIVES RE-INTERPRETED

Have you heard of the Woman so long under Ground
Have you heard of the Woman that Buckland has found
With her Bones of empyrial Hues?
O fair ones of modern Days, hang down your head
The Antediluvians rouged when Dead
Only granted in lifetime to you

Written by one of Buckland's students in 1823, possibly Philip Bury Duncan (1772–1863), later Keeper of the Ashmolean Museum, Oxford.

In 1823 William Buckland (1784–1856), theologian and Professor of Geology at Oxford University, excavated in Goat's Hole Cave, Paviland, on the Gower Peninsula, and found a skeleton stained red. He regarded the deposit as an intrusion, and rejecting it as proof of the existence of a fossil being, he first suggested that the bones were those of a customs officer murdered by smugglers. By the time he published his discovery a year later, the ochre-stained skeleton had become a 'painted lady' who had serviced the needs of the Roman garrison nearby. Following further excavations by William Sollas in 1912, the 'Red Lady' was reinterpreted as a ceremonial burial dating to the Upper Palaeolithic. In 1960, with radiocarbon dating, it was possible to date it to about 18,460 +/- 340 years ago, coinciding with the peak of the last Ice Age. The burial, now known to be male, has recently been reassessed by Professors Aldhouse-Green and Trinkhaus, and a refined radiocarbon date has been obtained of 25,840 +/- 280 years ago.

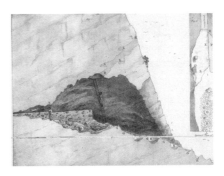

Section through the Paviland Cave from Buckland's Reliquiae Diluvianae (1823) showing the skeleton in sediments in which fossil bones are numerous. Buckland could not accept that the 'antediluvian' bones of animals such as mammoth and woolly rhinoceros from these sediments were the same age as the burial. According to his beliefs, they should have perished in Noah's flood.

The ritual burial at Paviland Cave, Gower, by Gino D'Achille (oil on board, about 1980). This painting was completed when the burial was thought to date to the period 35–28,000 BC. The body is shown for artistic convenience in a shallow grave, and red ochre powder is being poured over the body. The open tundra of the British Channel Plain is visible through the cave entrance. The body was originally found by the cave wall, and the theatrical arrangement of people in the ceremony is unlikely. Recent research suggests that the red ochre may have been applied to the clothing prior to the body being dressed; the ivory rods discovered with the burial were only found in short lengths, but have been interpreted in the painting as wands rather than blanks for an ivory workshop. Clear distinctions in the intensity of staining at the waist and ankle may reflect two-piece clothing and shoes.

Model of the ritual burial at Paviland cave created in 1996 on the basis of a reassessment of the archaeological evidence. When he died, he was about 25–30 years of age, and about 1.74m tall. Stable isotope analysis of the carbon and nitrogen in the bones has established that the diet contained an element of seafood. His DNA sequence corresponds to the commonest extant lineage in Europe and shows that our roots go back, not to the first farmers as used to be thought, but to the arrival of modern humans in Europe.

FACES: WE ARE OUR ANCESTORS

How have we changed through time? The tradition of re-creating likenesses is an ancient craft – some of the earliest attempts to re-create facial features by plastering skulls have been found at Jericho dating from the Neolithic period (about 7500–5500 BC). For the medieval and classical worlds, portrait painting and sculpture give some idea of the appearance of individuals, while early authors have provided a written record of people. Portraits may show something significant about the sitter's character or social standing, and the artist may have invested the picture with qualities the sitter did not possess, in order to flatter.

Many people in medieval and earlier western Europe probably looked much like those brought up in the countryside in the early twentieth century, away from urban influences. Changes in diet and sanitary and hygiene conditions have since brought about changes in weight, age of puberty, stature and health. The most obvious changes have been in hairstyle and clothing. Now, modern reconstructions show figures which more closely resemble ourselves in facial features, expressions and pose – a contrast with earlier perceptions of our ancestors.

Right: Katheryn of Berain, *by Adriaen van Cronenburgh (oil on panel, dated 1568). The portrait conveys both her appearance and her formidable character. Her left hand rests on a skull, which is not just a universal symbol of mortality, but also a demonstration that the artist understands the structure of the face and what lies beneath the skin: that the face is defined by the skull shape and details (with a detail of the skull from the portrait, above). (National Museum of Wales)*

The features of an individual face are determined by basic skull shape, the depth of tissue over the bone, and details such as facial hair and colour of eyes. Co-operation between forensic science and archaeology has led to two main methods of re-creating faces: sculptural and computerized. Sculptural facial reconstruction relies on musculature and soft-tissue data. This technique, pioneered in Britain by the Unit of Art in Medicine at the University of Manchester, is based on the anatomical methodology developed by Russian anthropologist Mikhail Gerasimov (1907–70) in relative isolation during the Cold War. His work became recognized in the West in the 1970s. A plaster cast of the skull is made for this procedure. Small circular pegs are inserted into drilled holes at precise locations, to indicate depth of muscle and tissue. Tissue depth is calculated using data based on age, sex and racial origin group of the individual. With pegs in place, individual muscles and layers of soft tissue are added. There are usually no clues about the size and shape of ears, or style of hair, but a general indication may be provided. The process brings together the work of numerous specialists, from dentists, radiologists and geneticists to archaeologists and facial anthropologists.

Musculature being added to plaster casts of skulls from Llanbedrgoch, Isle of Anglesey. (Unit of Art in Medicine, University of Manchester)

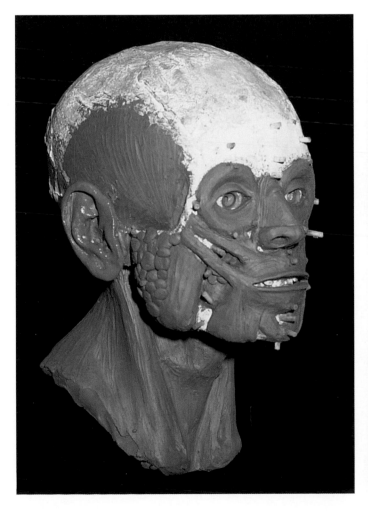
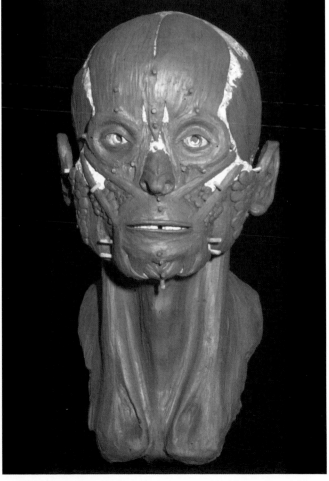

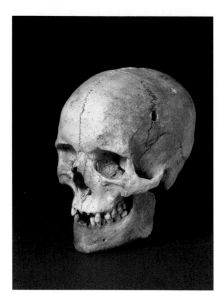

The human skull from the Penywyrlod burial chamber, Powys. (National Museum of Wales)

A PIONEER FARMER FROM THE NEOLITHIC

Computerized facial reconstruction, developed in recent years for reconstructive surgery and pioneered by University College Hospital, London, uses medical scanning techniques such as computed tomography (CT-scans).

The form of the skull is plotted by a low-power laser beam, and the 3D skeletal measurements stored on computer. A number of different faces of the same age and sex as the individual are scanned and merged to produce an 'average' face. This is then merged with the scan of the skull, adding appropriate muscle and tissue depths at key points. The resulting mask is theoretically very close to that of the true person, and may be redrawn. Conjectural details such as facial hair, wrinkles, complexion and eye colour can be added. Alternatively, a three-dimensional face can be created from a block of hard styrene foam by a computer-controlled milling machine.

The anatomical details of this Neolithic skull from the burial chamber at Penywyrlod, Powys, indicate that this man was probably in his mid- to late-20s when he died, about 3500 BC. He may have suffered minor osteoporosis (brittle bone disease) and had a scalp infection. He was a member of one of the first farming communities in Wales, and probably looked rather like ourselves.

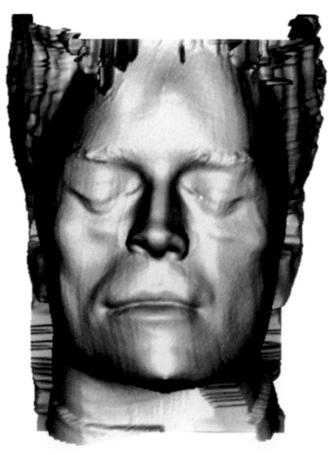

Computer image of the Penywyrlod face. (Past Forward Ltd, York Archaeological Trust)

The facial reconstruction based on the computerized image. (Past Forward Ltd, York Archaeological Trust)

DEATH MOST HORRID: HISTORY MADE HUMAN

Archaeologists may be called upon to establish the facts and circumstances of a particular event, in the manner of the forensic investigation of a crime scene. Reconstructing what may have happened is a cumulative process of understanding, which integrates the evidence from different sources to form a coherent story.

In 1998–99, an unexpected and puzzling discovery was made at the early medieval settlement at Llanbedrgoch, Isle of Anglesey. Five human skeletons were found in the upper fill of a ditch situated immediately outside the defensive wall of the settlement. The context and disposition of the burials suggested that they were the victims of violence, but what had happened and when? The bodies are of:

- A young woman, about 20 years old (burial 1)
- An adolescent, about 17 years old (burial 2)
- A double burial: an adult male, about 25–35 years old (burial 3) had been thrown directly on top of a child, about 10 years old (burial 4). The adult's wrists may have been tied behind his back, and he may have suffered a blow to the left eye with a sharp object.
- An older adult male, about 35–45 years old (burial 5) may also have had his wrists fastened in front of his body.

Refinements in the technique of radiocarbon dating (Accelerator Mass Spectrometry) now make it possible to date small samples of bone. Such dating from the Llanbedrgoch skeletons indicates that they were probably buried during the second half of the tenth century, at a period when Vikings on the Isle of Man

General view of the burials, lying in the upper fill of a ditch, Llanbedrgoch. (National Museum of Wales)

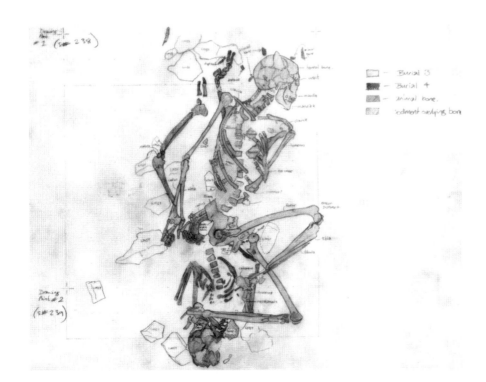

Analysis (above) of the skeleton plan (left) at Llanbedrgoch; the adult male (burial 3) lies on top of a child (burial 4). Both were buried at the same time. (National Museum of Wales)

A

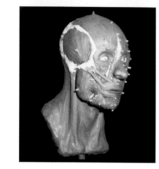

B

effectively controlled Gwynedd, and may have had bases on Anglesey. The precise circumstances of their deaths may never be known, but they may have been the victims of military activity by Vikings in their search for wealth, perhaps in the form of hostages or slaves.

Four of the faces have been re-created by facial anthropologist Caroline Wilkinson. Research suggests that it is possible to re-assemble a fragmented skull and re-model missing areas with good accuracy. The Llanbedrgoch skulls were all crushed, and during re-assembly missing areas had to be remodelled using modelling wax. Forensic anthropology can point to a skeleton's deviation from normal appearance, and the presence of injuries. In the case of the Llanbedrgoch skulls, all show a number of similar features, which include horizontal eye fissures, supra-orbital notches (above the eyes), ambiguous nasal guttering, square jaws and adherent ears (no lobes) and a wide flattened nasal spine. Some of these features suggest a genetic relationship between the skulls, either familial or because the individuals originate from a small gene pool.

C

D

Above: *Stages in the facial reconstruction procedure: (A) reassembled skull of an adult male, 25–35 years old (burial 3, Llanbedrgoch), (B) musculature on plaster cast, (C) clay version (minus hair), (D) wax version. The colour of the eyes, skin and hair are conjectural; the hair style is based on a description written some 200 years later by Gerald of Wales. (A, B Unit of Art in Medicine, University of Manchester; C ,D National Museum of Wales)*

Right: *The facial reconstructions of (from left) burials 3, 5, 4 and 2, Llanbedrgoch, by Dr Caroline Wilkinson (2002), cast in bronze. (National Museum of Wales)*

HISTORY ALIVE

Any attempt to relive the remote past is destined to failure, because the knowledge and experience of previous generations are denied to us. To place modern man into a prehistoric context, given the limitations of our knowledge, is only to observe how modern people may react both to the conditions and to each other.

Peter Reynolds (from *Iron-Age Farm. The Butser Experiment*, 1979)

To what extent can history be brought to life? Living history has its origins in the historical play and the pageant, delighting audiences with a blend of spectacle and history. Social and political developments during the late nineteenth and early twentieth centuries, such as the promotion of education and literacy, had considerable impact on the popular representation of the past. The spectacular National Pageant of Wales was performed in Sophia Garden Fields, Cardiff, between 26 July and 7 August 1909. With a script by the writer and adventurer Robert Scourfield Mills ('Owen Rhoscomyl'), the 'stirring events' depicted began with an episode in which Caratacus appealed to the king of the Silures for assistance in repelling the Romans. The educational value of the event was recognized by the Chief Inspector of Education who involved teachers and scholars from most schools in Wales, so that 60,000 school children had been booked seats at the dress rehearsals three weeks before the Pageant opened. The Pageant armour, made of papier maché, was carefully researched and at the time was considered to be 'the most realistic assembly of ancient war-like material ever seen at a mimic display of arms'. Needless to say, the entertainment value was also appreciated at the time.

Mr Morgan Williams of St Donat's Castle played the part of 'Prince Llywelyn the Great' in the National Pageant of Wales (1909). Members of county families assumed the roles of historic characters. (C. Corn)

A scene from the National Pageant of Wales, in which some 500 of the 'most prominent football players in Wales' who take the part of 'unkempt and unarmoured Welsh clansmen under their redoubtable chief, Ivor Bach' prepare to storm Cardiff Castle (AD 1158). (C. Corn)

How a tenth-century ringed pin fastened cloaks. Similar pins have been found at the Viking-period settlement at Llanbedrgoch, Isle of Anglesey. This replica is worn by a member of the living history group Cwmwd Îal.

One of the first battle re-enactment societies to be formed in Britain was the Sealed Knot Society (1967). There are now many such groups, such as the Wars of the Roses Federation, The English Civil War Society and the Napoleonic Association, and their interests include the rivalries, power, ideologies and struggles of different periods. In recent years, the membership of re-enactment and living history groups has increased, in parallel with a growth of public interest in social rather than political history. Members of these groups gather information from diverse sources to re-create as authentically as possible the costume and equipment of the past, in many cases using the same materials and methods of manufacture. This can help answer practical questions raised by archaeologists, and plays an important part in correcting mistaken impressions of the past. Their public displays offer a valuable form of experimental archaeology, where clothing and equipment can be tested, and long-extinct activities demonstrated, whether preparing tallow lamps, using plants and vegetable dyes, or writing on wax tablets. The efforts of early re-enactors have informed successors who have sought to resurrect skills, and the demand for their products has grown, enabling some to employ 'apprentices' and hand on their traditional skills. As noted by many commentators, re-creating the past in the present is not easy, and however brilliant, can never be absolutely accurate. There are limitations to reliving the past, as demonstrated by various televised projects.

The medieval 'mess hall' at Tretower Court, Powys: showing visitors what kind of food may have been prepared about 500 years ago.

Right: *The Ermine Street Guard at the Roman amphitheatre, Caerleon. This re-enactment group, formed in 1972, has established a long tradition of public displays at the Roman legionary fortress, Caerleon. It is committed to researching and reproducing the equipment and drill of the Roman Imperial Army of the late first century AD.*

Below and left: *Re-enactment of the Battle of St Fagans (1648) at the Museum of Welsh Life, St Fagans (1998). These re-enactors belong to the Sealed Knot Society, one of the first re-enactment groups to be formed, in 1967. At first 'musters', the costume was ingenious if not authentic (bonded velvet uniforms, recycled rubber boots, and tennis balls for cannon shot), but with the growth of the society, their clothing and armoury have been carefully researched, and are now made by specialist craftsmen.*

Our Past in the Future

Developing technology should make it easier to reconcile our slowly evolving perception of our past with the rapidly changing view created by advancing research. What we cannot understand now, we may understand in the future, and computer-based technology will make the presentation of new information easier.

Non-text based forms of communication, such as CD-ROMs, touch-screen videos, animatronics and virtual reality reconstructions are being increasingly used. More sophisticated computer software will make it easier to question and update the images created, and provide fresh or alternative interpretations.

Reconstructing human beings will become increasingly accurate. New information on soft tissue thicknesses for a wide range of racial types will lead to more detailed facial reconstructions, particularly now that data can be obtained from living people. Some museums have incorporated facial reconstructions into life-size dioramas, reinforcing the scientific basis for such visual spectacles. Virtual reality sculpting is even being developed, opening up the possibility of animating reconstructed faces.

The range of full-size simulations will continue to grow, including 'ecomuseums' which attempt to interpret the whole landscape by examining the relationship between people and their environment, and archaeological parks which allow the public to 'experience' re-created historic settings. Just as nineteenth-century historical painting enabled the public magically to 'see' and appreciate visions of the past, advances in the range of techniques of presentation and interpretation will inform us of a past which will continue to surprise, entertain, educate and enthral.

The replica of the 1925 logboat from Llan-gors Lake with the crannog in the background (1993). (National Museum of Wales)

Llan-gors crannog, Powys, about AD 900, based on the 1989–93 excavations. The logboat is a copy of that found in the lake in 1925. This montage by Tony Daly (2001) combines scanned line drawings with photographs, using computer software. (National Museum of Wales)